Revise and Test

# Business Englis.. _

**David Whitehead** MA BEd

*Series Adviser:* Geoffrey Whitehead Bsc(Econ)

**Pitman**

PITMAN PUBLISHING LIMITED
128 Long Acre, London WC2E 9AN

A Longman Group Company

© David Whitehead 1986

First published in Great Britain 1986

**British Library Cataloguing in Publication Data**
Whitehead, David
    Business English.—(Revise and test) 2
    1. English language—Business English
    I. Title    II. Series
    808'.066651021        PE1115

    ISBN 0-273-02470-1

Printed and bound in Great Britain at The Bath Press, Avon

By the same author:
*Pitman Business Correspondence*

# Contents

# Using this Revise and Test booklet

**1** The 'Revise and Test' series is in question and answer form. It will teach you everything you need to know about your particular syllabus. The questions are detailed and rigorous, and cannot be answered always with one word. It follows that the first time you go over a topic you will be learning the material rather than testing yourself. It is not just a self-testing book, but a self-teaching book too!

**2** The first time you study a topic you may need to go over it two or three times. Then put a tick against the topic number in the check list at the back of the book.

**3** Subsequently you should revise the topic at intervals, especially just before a monthly test or an examination. Each time you revise it put in a further tick.

**4** If you find a topic particularly difficult, put a ring round the number. This will remind you to do it again soon. Practice makes perfect.

**5** Finally remember that learning facts is relatively easy. Applying them in written work is more difficult. Each topic has one piece of written work and you should find others from textbooks and past examination papers. Remember the saying 'Writing maketh an exact man'. Don't worry about who is going to mark your written work. You can appraise it for yourself! Keep writing!

*Note:* This is Book 2 of *Revise and Test Business English*. *Revise and Test Business English Book 1* is obtainable from all good booksellers.

# 1 Memoranda

**1 What is a memo (or memorandum)?**

It is a short note sent *within* a business organisation.

**2 What is the function of a memorandum?**

It may be written to convey instructions, provide information, or to remind the recipient about something. (The word memorandum was originally Latin and meant 'a thing which is to be remembered'.)

**3 How does the layout of a memorandum differ from that of a letter?**

When writing a memorandum you do not include a salutation or a subscription. Most firms have a printed memo slip, or at least a standardised form for writing memos. Included in the memorandum should be the name of the person sending it, and that of the recipient. You may also include a heading stating the subject matter, and the date and even the time at which the memorandum was written. An example is given in Fig. 1.1.

```
From:   General Manager                        Date 14 October
To:     Personnel Manager                      Time 14.30 hrs

                 Re: Visit of Local Councillors

Please arrange for a reception in the board room for five local
councillors who wish to discuss the Youth Employment Scheme, at
2 p.m. on 18th October.
```

**Fig. 1.1  A memorandum**

**4 What should be included in the memorandum?**

It is only a short note, so a memorandum should only deal with one main point. If you need to communicate two separate points, it would be better to send two memoranda.

**5 What must you remember when writing a memorandum?**

As with letter writing you must write simply and clearly. Avoid long, complicated sentences and unnecessary vocabulary. Keep your memorandum brief and to the point. Keep the sentences short and factual – as in the example in Fig. 1.2.

---

### MEMORANDUM

*From:* Richard Jones                                    *Extension:* 248
*To:*    Peter Gold (Progress Chaser)              *Date:* 17 December 19--

---

Re Order 2785 for Doha. I see from the Journal of Commerce today that the Silver Crescent line ferry 'Star of the Sea' was lost in the Mediterranean yesterday. She was due to handle this cargo to Doha on her next trip. Can you get on to the agents and find out the position please so we don't let Doha down? These units are urgently required for their construction project. Please keep me informed of the position.

                                    Dick

---

**Fig. 1.2 A memo dealing with an emergency**

**6 What is a three-part NCR memo set?**

It is a memo set made up of an original plus two copies which have been coated with minute invisible globules of ink. The memo is written on the top part of the top copy and as it writes the pen breaks the globules of ink on the copies below to give two further copies. The sender tears off the top copy and retains it. The two lower copies are sent to the addressee, who writes a reply on the lower half of the memo. This naturally produces a copy below it. The

| | addressee separates the two copies, keeps one and sends the other back to the original sender. |
|---|---|
| **7 Why is it called an NCR set?** | Because NCR means 'no carbon required'. |

**Written Exercise:** *Write a memo to Teresa Lorensen asking her if she has heard about the problem with the funeral consignment by air from Philadelphia. The freighter has been delayed with engine trouble and the parents of the deceased person must be informed. Postpone the funeral by 48 hours. Please apologise and say we did warn them. A personal visit seems appropriate in the circumstances – but it must be done this afternoon. Use your own name, invent an extension number, date and time.*

*Go over the topic again until you are sure of all the answers. Then tick it off on the check list at the back of the book.*

# 2 Preparing and planning a report

| | |
|---|---|
| **1 Are reports important in the modern business world?** | Yes, they are essential. They can provide information, make recommendations, give advice, analyse data and perform many other valuable tasks which the modern businessman/woman needs. |
| **2 What form does a report take?** | There is no one set form for a report. The style of report will vary according to the material you wish to communicate and the person who is to read the report. It may be long or short, formal or informal, a memorandum report or a letter report, etc. However, regardless of the form the report takes, you should follow the same process in its preparation, planning and writing. |
| **3 What should you be clear about before you begin to prepare a report?** | (a) Why am I writing it? (b) What is it about? (c) Who is going to read it? |

**4  Why do reports get written?**

Usually because there is some problem, and a person or committee in charge of such events sets up an investigation team to examine it.

**5  What do we call the resolution setting up the team?**

It is called the 'terms of reference'. It appoints the team, and a team leader. It outlines the problem to be investigated, and sets a time limit for the team to report back.

**6  What does the team need to know before it can start work?**

It must know the purpose of the report. The members need to decide, before they begin, *the area they intend to cover*. This will probably involve discussion with the party for whom they are preparing the report.

For example, a report about a fire in a warehouse will present the facts about the incident, but the purpose of the report may be to lodge an insurance claim, or to make recommendations about safety regulations.

**7  Why do we need to consider who is going to read the report?**

Because this will affect its form and style. Think about the reader when choosing vocabulary and arranging ideas. Is the report being written for technical specialists or for people with limited technical knowledge? Always bear in mind the reader's needs, knowledge and requirements.

**8  How do you collect the material for your report?**

Once you have decided on the terms of reference for the report, the time-consuming, but essential, activity of gathering information must take place. This may involve research, analysis of data, on site inspection, etc. Gradually you should build up a collection of information, some of which you will use while rejecting the rest as not relevant.

**9  What is the danger here in analysing data collected?**

You must not be too hasty in dismissing information unless it is clearly irrelevant to the subject of the report.

**10  Describe the analysis of evidence**

It is a process of selecting appropriate material for the report. As you gather information, your **conclusions** and **recommendations** should emerge. You separate them from the rest of the material. Then you begin to select the relevant evidence which will support your conclusions and recommendations. You must try to find the right balance of evidence, as too much will obscure the point you are trying to make, and too little will leave you with unfounded opinions and unjustified recommendations. This **balance** will only develop with practice. The information you select will form the main part of the report.

**11  What should you do once you have selected the material?**

The next task is to arrange the information in the most logical form. This **planning stage** is crucial for the development of an effective report, for if the information is presented in an illogical order, the reader will not be able to follow the ideas and evidence easily, and the report will not be clear. The material should be subdivided and a detailed plan prepared.

**12  What might be a likely order of items, for example, in a report about the movement of a firm's head office from the capital to a new town in the countryside?**

*Report on Desirability of Moving the Head Office from Capital City to Newtown* (a) Terms of reference of the investigating team. (b) Introduction – outlining the problem. (c) The condition of the present building and the projected cost of renovation and continued occupation in Capital City. (d) The arguments in favour of moving to Newtown, mentioning: (i) Help offered by the Newtown authority; (ii) Suitability of the premises and location generally; (iii) Staffing advantages; (iv) Estimated savings on rent, rates or other taxation; (v) Proximity of proposed head office to main factory in Newtown. (e) Disadvantages of move: (i) cost of new building; (ii) advantages of staying in Capital City. (f) Conclusions and recommendations. (g) Appendices of evidence collated.

**13 List the main tasks in preparing and planning a report**

(a) Know *why* you are writing the report. (b) Know the *area* your report is supposed to cover. (c) Know *for whom* you are writing the report. (d) Gather your *information*. (e) Decide on your *conclusions* and *recommendations*. (f) *Select relevant information* to support your conclusions and recommendations. (g) If necessary explain why you reject other evidence. (h) *Plan* your report by organising your material into the most logical order.

When you have done this, you are ready to begin writing your report.

**Written Exercise:** *You are a referee at a match which you were forced to abandon because of an invasion of the pitch by spectators. The incident became very ugly and menacing, with young children present in a crowd where there was considerable violent movement, groups pursuing other groups, etc.*

*Write a report for the governing body of the sport about the reasons for abandoning the match.*

*Go over the topic again until you are sure of all the answers. Then tick it off on the check list at the back of the book.*

# 3 Writing a report

**1 What are the three important elements to consider when writing a report?**

They are **structure**, the **language** and the **presentation** of the report.

**2 Why is the structure of the report important?**

It gives the report a sound framework, so that the reader can follow the report more easily. The usual structure of a report is as follows: (a) the title page; (b) contents; (c) summary; (d) introduction; (e) the body of the report; (f) conclusions; (g) recommendations; (h) appendices; (i) acknowledgements, references and bibliography; (j) index.

**3 What should be included on the title page?**

The title, stating the central theme of the report, the author's name, the recipient's name, the date and a reference number where appropriate.

**4 What is the function of the table of contents?**

It lists all the main sections in the report, with subdivisions and page numbers.

**5 Why is a summary included early in the report?**

It tells the reader briefly the contents of the body of the report, giving him/her a quick insight into the subject matter. In some cases a businessman may only have time to read the summary and the recommendations; so it is important that the summary gives an accurate presentation in a concise form of the main ideas expressed in the report. Even though it appears early in the report the summary should not be written until the main report has been completed.

**6 What information should be included in the introduction?**

In the introduction, you are preparing the reader for the body of the report. You should mention: (a) the terms of reference of the report – that is the area the report covers, and the reasons for its preparation; (b) the name of the author of the report; (c) the name of the people for whom the report is being written; (d) the general background to the subject of the report, but not in great detail.

**7 What is the first part of the report you should write?**

You should write the main body of the report first. All the information should have already been selected and arranged; so now the task is to write it out in good English (which is dealt with later in this unit). If the report is long and complex, the reader might find it easier to follow if a conclusion is written at the end of each subsection.

**8 How do you decide on your conclusions?**

These must be based on the information you have presented in the main body of the report. If you have included a conclusion in each subsection you must repeat it in the main 'conclusions' section of the report.

**9 How important are the recommendations?**

They are important, because they are the reason most reports are written. If you have done your work thoroughly you should now be the expert on the subject. The person for whom you wrote the report will want to know your suggestions for resolving the problems which your analysis has been considering. Your recommendations should follow logically from your conclusions and attempt to persuade the reader to follow the course of action which should be taken.

**10 What is the function of the appendix?**

An appendix has two main functions. Firstly, it is where any supplementary data which supports ideas expressed in the main body of the report may be placed. Illustrative material such as graphs, charts, statistics, etc., may be included here. Secondly, it may be necessary to up-date the report, by including the latest information. In order to avoid writing the whole report again, the new material may be included in the appendix. In addition, the appendix may include a glossary of technical terms and a list of abbreviations used.

**11 What are acknowledgements?**

This is the section in which you thank those people who have helped you to draw up the report. You may prefer to do this after the contents page.

**12 Why is it necessary to include references and a bibliography?**

The references list refers to material not easily available, such as research papers etc., to which you have referred in the report. The bibliography is a list of the books and articles used in the process of compiling the report. It is usual to state the title of the book, the full name of the author, plus the name of the publisher and the date of publication of the edition you have used.

**13 Why is it important to think about the language of your report?**

As with all business communications one important quality of good report writing is that the reader can understand what you are saying. There are several important skills you can learn which will make your report clearer. Some of them have already been mentioned earlier in this book, and they are dealt with more fully in Topic 8 on *The Style and Tone of Business Writing*.

**14 Briefly list the skills of good writing**

(a) Have a specific purpose in mind and stick to the point. (b) Always remember who your reader is and adopt an appropriate tone and choice of vocabulary to suit the reader. (c) Be accurate in your choice of words. (d) Be concise in expression; do not ramble or repeat yourself. (e) Be clear: there is no place for ambiguity in a report. (f) Keep your vocabulary simple where possible; do not use long words merely to impress the reader. (g) Unless you are writing a scientific or technical report, which will be read only by a specialist group, avoid jargon. (h) Avoid the use of clichés (words which have been over-used and have lost their precise meanings). (i) Keep your sentences short and simple wherever possible. Long, rambling sentences full of subordinate clauses may only confuse your reader. (j) Paragraphs, too, should be short where possible. Always remember to use a key sentence. (k) Punctuate your report accurately, so that the meaning is made clear to the reader. (l) Where you are unsure about the spelling of a word, check it in a dictionary.

**15 Is your job completed once you have written the report?**

No. The next task is to revise the first draft of your report. It is advisable to leave this job for a while, perhaps a day, so that when you return to the report you can have a fresh look at it. As a result, you may see errors or weaknesses which you might have missed if you had started your revision immediately after completing the first draft.

**16 What should you be looking for when revising your report?**

(a) Errors of grammar, expression, spelling, punctuation, etc. (b) Any unnecessary repetition or irrelevant material. (c) Faulty or poorly developed argument. (d) A lack of evidence to support your conclusions. (e) Important information omitted. (f) Ambiguity.

Above all, you should be checking to make sure that the report is easy to read, develops in a logical manner, is well supported by evidence and is clearly set out.

**17 How important is the presentation of the report?**

First impressions are always important. While good presentation will not disguise a weak report, poor presentation may well deter the reader. Clear presentation, with headings and numbering, helps to break down the subject matter of the report, making it easier for the reader to assimilate.

**18 What should you be aware of when considering the layout of your report?**

Remember not to make your page too crowded, as this looks unattractive and makes the report more difficult to read. Break the reading material down by: (a) using clear headings; (b) having double space type; (c) using wide margins.

**19 What is the value of headings?**

Headings act as signposts, guiding the reader through the report. You should devise different styles of heading, depending on the importance of the subject matter. For example, a heading for a major section of the report might be in capital letters:

### ADVANTAGES OF SITING MICROPROCESSING PLANT IN SINGAPORE

A subheading might mix capital and lower case lettering:

1.1 *Labour Force*

A paragraph heading might use a capital letter for the first word, and thereafter use lower case lettering:

1.1.1 Skilled and experienced labour force.

There is no hard and fast rule about the style of heading to adopt. The important point to remember is that once you have started with a system of headings, you should be consistent and stick to it. Many organisations lay down an agreed 'house style' to be used by all members of staff. Get to know the 'house style' and use it at all times.

**20  How should you number your report?**

As with headings, there is no set rule on this. But frequent and consistent numbering is important, as it helps you to organise your material, and aids the reader's comprehension of the different sections of the report. The decimal system as used in the examples in Question 19 is popular, and helps to avoid confusion, especially in longer reports.

**21  When should the report be typed?**

There is a strong case for the report to be typed before revision, as it is easier to look objectively at script than at a handwritten report. Also, it gives the writer a break from the report, so that he/she can revise it with a fresh mind. However, if it is necessary to alter much of the report, the typist must be given adequate time before the due date for submitting the report. The use of a word processor takes much of the strain from a typist when retyping is necessary.

**Written Exercise:** *The safety officer, Tom Jones, has called for a report on the circumstances in which an employee died as a result of touching a live cable brought down when a pylon was damaged in the car park. You have been asked to chair the ad hoc committee set up to investigate, and to write the report. Draw up the title page and the introduction to this report. Invent any names or other informatioon you need.*

*Go over the topic again until you are sure of all the answers. Then tick it off on the check list at the back of the book.*

# 4  Making notes

**1  Are there many situations when a person involved in business would need to make notes?**

Yes, there are many such situations. For example, you may be required to take the minutes of a meeting or you may have to extract information from books or trade journals in order to gather material for a report you are preparing. Both of these activities demand skilled note-taking.

**2 What are the advantages of taking notes?**

(a) They provide a written record of what has been said in a meeting or seminar. (b) They help you to understand what you are listening to or reading, because they focus your attention on the main points of a speech or written passage. (c) They can help you to learn more easily, because information is clearly broken down into small units and simplified.

**3 What are the basic rules about taking notes?**

(a) Notes should be as brief as possible and should concentrate on the main ideas. (b) Other details and examples should only be included if they are important supporting material. (c) A system of heading and numbering will help to make your notes clearer (refer to Topic 3 on *Writing a Report*).

**4 How do you begin to take notes from a written passage?**

Taking accurate notes depends on a clear understanding of the passage being read. Read the passage thoroughly, several times if necessary, until you have grasped the main points.

**5 How can you spot the main points?**

This can only come with practice, but you can help yourself by: (a) learning to recognise the key sentence (see Topic 3 *Revise and Test Business English 1*) in a paragraph which expresses the main idea contained in the paragraph; (b) being aware of connectors (see Topic 11 *Revise and Test Business English 1*) – words like *therefore, however, but, or, although*, etc. – which tell you the direction the passage is about to take.

**6 What do you do next?**

(a) If you are using a book which is your own property, take a pencil and underline the main points with a straight line. Underline any minor points with a wavy line. (b) When you have been through the complete passage decide on a suitable title for your notes. (c) Make a list of headings, one heading for each section of your notes. Each heading should be numbered. (d) Under each heading, you may have a series of subheadings if the passage is particularly long or complicated. These should also be numbered. (e) Under each subheading list the points you have gleaned from the passage. These do not need to be written in full sentences, but should be in brief note form only. You do not have to worry about punctuation or grammar, so long as you can understand what you have written. An example is given below:

*Movement through Customs –Simplified Customs Procedure (SCP)*
(a)  Pre-entry not necessary.
(b)  Documentation based on SCP approved document – may be SSN, CMR note, CIM note, C271 etc., EC1 number essential.
(c)  Documents to loader, who seeks authority to load from export officer.
(d)  C273 or other entry made out later — must have same EC1 number as SCP document.
(e)  Must reach Southend within 14 days.

**7 Why is taking notes of a speech more difficult than taking notes from a written passage?**

(a) Generally our formal education teaches us to read, but less attention is paid to teaching children to listen. As a result we do not always listen carefully to what is being said, and consequently we misunderstand what we are told. (b)

Also, the written word is there for us to see again and again. If we do not understand part of the passage, we can read it repeatedly until we do understand it. But in a speech, the word is spoken and then lost for ever (unless we have a tape-recorder). Moreover, we may be so busy writing a note on what the speaker has just said that we miss what he/she is saying now. (c) Finally, our understanding of a speech will be affected by the quality of the speaker. Whereas a good speaker will know how to vary the pace, tone and volume of his voice to aid understanding, a poor speaker may only confuse or bore the listeners.

**8 How should you take notes on a speech or discussion?**

Basically the layout of the notes will be exactly the same as for notes on a written passage, with headings, subheadings, numbering etc. You may need to tidy up your notes when the speech has finished, rewriting them, adding headings, etc., when you can look more objectively at the speech as a whole. However, there are listening skills that you will need to develop in order to be able to make good notes on a speech.

**9 What listening skills do you need to acquire?**

(a) *Concentrate* on what the speaker is saying. Do not merely relax and let the words wash over you, but listen attentively. (b) *Be aware of the speaker's delivery.* His/her voice may change its tone, volume or pace. These are clues which help the listener to interpret the words more correctly. Inflection (the way the voice rises and falls in a sentence) also affects the meaning of what is being said. You must train yourself to be sensitive to the way the speaker uses his/her voice. (c) Listen

15

for connectors or signal words. These are vital in a good speech, because they prepare the listener for what is to come next. Phrases like 'to come back to the point made earlier' or 'if I could move on to something else' are useful guides which you need to take note of when listening to a speech. (d) Try to grasp the structure of the speech, and to organise your notes accordingly.

**10  How can you learn these listening skills?**

Listen to a discussion or documentary programme on the radio. Have a pencil and paper ready, and try taking notes as you listen. Perhaps you could do this exercise with a friend, and then compare the notes you have taken.

**Written Exercise:** *Listen to the next news bulletin on the radio or television and make notes of each item. Number them afterwards and discover how many items were considered newsworthy.*

*Go over the topic again until you are sure of all the answers. Then tick it off on the check list at the back of the book.*

# 5  Business meetings – 1: agenda and minutes

**1  What English skills are required in a business meeting?**

There are many different skills needed to conduct a meeting effectively. They include sending out a notice for all to attend, the writing of the agenda, the taking of the minutes, the ability to speak clearly and relevantly, being able to argue your point of view, etc. Some of these skills will be discussed in the next chapter.

**2  When circulating a notice to members of a committee, what details should be included?**

(a) The date, time and venue (the place where the meeting will be held). (b) The purpose of the meeting – unless an agenda is enclosed, or is mentioned as 'agenda to follow'. (c) The minutes of the previous meeting unless already circulated. (d) The circulation of the notice – so that members know who else is expected to attend.

**3  What is an agenda?**

A detailed list of items to be discussed. It forms the basis for the conduct of the meeting; the chairman dealing with the items in the sequence given in the agenda and moving on to the next item when the discussion on a particular item is concluded.

**4  Certain items come at the very beginning of an agenda. What are they?**

(a) *Apologies for absence*   (If you are going to be absent you should send the Chairman a memo explaining why). Last minute apologies may be conveyed at the meeting on your behalf by a member who *is* in attendance. (b) *Minutes of the previous meeting*   These should be read out – which can be a tedious business – but if they have been circulated previously anyone may propose 'that the minutes be taken as read'. (c) *Matters arising*   These are matters arising from the minutes – members may want to know what happened about some decision taken at the last meeting, etc. The Chairman may halt such discussion at once if the matter arising appears on the agenda lower down – because a full discussion of developments will take place at that point in the meeting. (d) *Correspondence*   Any important letters received since the previous meeting.

**5  What comes next?**

The main items on the agenda – the chief topics to be discussed at this meeting.

## 6 How is an agenda prepared?

(a) The secretary will prepare the agenda after liaison with the Chairman who will have a strong influence over the items to be discussed at a particular meeting. (b) The introductory items – apologies, etc., always appear. (c) The Chairman will usually have 2 or 3 items for the agenda based on follow-up procedures from earlier meetings. He/she will also usually know of new items that have arisen in the meantime. (d) Other members who wish to have an item discussed should draw it to the attention of the secretary – usually a deadline would be set of, say, 2 weeks before the meeting. The secretary would then draw it to the chairman's attention. If not accepted as an agenda item, it could still be raised under AOB – Any Other Business. (e) The secretary will then draw up a draft agenda which the Chairman may revise – perhaps by changing the order of items, etc. (f) Finally, the amended agenda will be duplicated and circulated.

## 7 What are the final items on most agendas?

(a) *Any other business* – usually written AOB. This gives an opportunity for any member to raise any point he/she likes. It is usually used for brief items which can be dealt with quickly – for example to acquaint the committee with the dates and times of other activities being arranged by other departments.
(b) *Date of next meeting*   This is a good opportunity to fill in a date in everyone's diary before it gets too congested.

## 8 Should the agenda be followed?

If the agenda has been carefully prepared, there should be no need to deviate from it. However, if someone does wish to take a point out of order (perhaps because they are forced to leave early) this should only be done if the meeting agrees to it. If anyone wishes to introduce a topic not mentioned on the agenda, this should be done in the final section of the meeting, *Any Other Business.*

**9 How important is the Chairman of a meeting?**

The Chairman has a vital role to play in the running of a meeting. His/her basic task is to maintain order, for without it, the meeting is likely to degenerate into a number of private discussions or arguments with little being achieved. The Chairman has to ensure that everyone has a fair chance to speak, limiting those who speak for too long and encouraging members who usually say nothing at all, He must be able to guide the discussion, ensuring that what is being said is relevant to the topic being discussed. It is important that the person chosen to be Chairman has a good knowledge of meeting procedures, so that he/she can make rulings when necessary.

**10 What is meant by the phrase 'through the chair, please'?**

Anyone who speaks at a meeting must speak to the meeting as a whole and not to an individual. To do this we address all remarks to the chairman. Thus it would be wrong to say: 'But Peter, I can't agree there because ...'. We have to speak through the chair, and say 'Mr Chairman, some of us would disagree with Peter Brown on this point because ...'.

**11 What are the minutes of a meeting?**

The minutes are an abbreviated record of what was said during a meeting. They will usually be taken by an experienced secretary, called the Minuting Secretary, who will not only be able to follow the discussion and note what is said, but will also be objective in recording the minutes – that is he/she will word the minutes in such a way as to avoid personal viewpoints.

**12  Who should take the minutes if an experienced secretary is not available?**

Taking the minutes of a meeting requires a number of advanced language skills, and it is important that the person chosen to record the minutes is capable of performing them. He/she must also be impartial, favouring neither side in a discussion, so that the minutes will be fair and accurate. The Chairman will usually select such a person from the group who are available.

**13  What skills are required in the taking of minutes?**

The person taking the minutes must be able to listen intelligently to the discussion. This demands concentration and a high degree of thoughtfulness. As the recorder listens he/she must be making a *mental summary* of what is said; this will become the basis of the minutes. To do this effectively, the minute-taker must be able to distinguish between the important points being made and the irrelevant or trivial comments. This is a complex task, especially when the summary is being made from the spoken, rather than the written, word. The recorder will need to be aware of **oral indications** which suggest when something important is being said, such as the stressing of points, or a change of tone and pace in what the speaker is saying. Also **discourse markers** (phrases like 'However', 'Furthermore', 'what I am trying to say is . . .' etc.) may assist the secretary.

**14  What are the chief points to remember when taking minutes?**

(a) A verbatim report of everything that is said is rarely required. (b) The minutes will start with a brief description of the meeting, the names of those present with the Chairman first and the officers last – ordinary members in between. A list of apologies for absence. (c) A note that the minutes were read, or taken as read, and were signed by the Chairman as a true record. (d) Matters arising should be noted. (e) Correspondence may include noteworthy items. (f) Then come the agenda items in turn, with a careful note of any resolutions, amendments, and decisions. If any duty is imposed upon, or voluntarily assumed, by any member, a note should be made and the matter can then be followed up. (g) Any other business, including the date of the next meeting.

**15 What type of language should be used when drawing up the minutes?**

Temperate language, which will not 'colour' the minutes. For example, to record 'a violent discussion arose' would not be appropriate. 'A lively debate followed' would be a better choice of words.

**16 What is the custom with regard to capital letters in minutes?**

It is usual to capitalise all names and official positions, such as Chairman, Secretary, Treasurer, etc.

**17 Is it important to take the minutes of a meeting?**

Yes it is. They provide a permanent record of the decisions taken at a meeting. It may be necessary to refer back to the minutes at some time in the future, to see how decisions were arrived at. A typical set of minutes is shown in Fig. 5.1.

**18 Does the style of the minutes ever change?**

The minutes can vary. They may be merely a record of the decision made, or they can be a more detailed account of the discussion leading up to decisions. At times, the minutes may be a full *verbatim* report, that is a word for word record of everything that was said, but this is very rare. The best example is *Hansard*, the reports of Parliamentary meetings.

<u>Safety Committee Meeting – ABC Ltd</u>

<u>Minutes of a meeting held at 11.00 a.m., Friday, 26th September, 1986</u>
<u>in the Recreation Annexe</u>

Members Present    Mr. R. T. Jones, Director (Chairman)
                       Mr. B. Jones (Safety Officer)
                       Mrs. J. Wright (Restaurant Manageress)
                       Mr. B. Peters (Works Representative)
                       Miss P. Schofield (Office Representative)
                       Mr. P. Whyte (Secretary, Transport Subcommittee)
                       Miss J. Dee (Minuting Secretary)
                       Messrs. J. Whyte, P. Tripp, C. Morrison and B. Lucas
                       (Departmental Representatives)

Apologies      All were present on this occasion.

35/86   <u>Minutes of Previous Meeting</u>
           The minutes of the meeting held on Friday, 27th June, 1986 were
           taken as read, adopted and signed by the Chairman.

36/86   <u>Matters Arising</u>
29/86   Mr Jones reported that he and Mrs Wright attended the
           funeral of R. Lambourne who was killed in a canteen accident.
           The widow's welfare had been properly cared for.

37/86   <u>Transport Report</u>
           An account of the new service bay was given after the redesign
           made necessary by the petrol pump fire. Three complaints about
           transport safety had been investigated and the details were
           explained. All three had been resolved by reprimands to staff.

38/86   <u>Fire Precautions</u>
           Mr Whyte reported that the training scheme for young HGV drivers
           was fully operational and promised to be successful. An official
           inspection had been arranged for November 7th and a full team
           from the Department of Transport was expected.

**Fig. 5.1 Minutes of a Safety**
**Committee meeting**

39/86 <u>Letter of Complaint</u>
A matter raised concerning fire appliances in the firm's motor
transport department was agreed to need thorough investigation.

    It was <u>RESOLVED</u> that a subcommittee be formed
    (Messrs R. T. Jones, B. Jones, B. Lucas to
    serve).

40/86 <u>First Aid Training</u>
A complaint about inadequate first-aid facilities was received
from the Works Representative.

    It was <u>RESOLVED</u> that this matter be raised at
    Board Room level and the Chairman arrange its
    inclusion in the Board Meeting Agenda. Mr B.
    Peters was delegated to attend and explain
    the matter, with a view to an approved training
    programme.

41/86 <u>A.O.B.</u>
There being no other business the meeting adjourned at 12.50 p.m.

<u>Date of Next Meeting</u>
    Friday, 6th March 1987 at 10.30 a.m. in the Recreation Annexe.

                        Chairman: 6th March 1987 . . . . . . . . . .

**19 What should the Minuting Secretary do after the meeting is over?**

The person taking the minutes will have a shorthand record of the minutes. These should be transcribed, in clear English with appropriate headings and subheadings. These draft minutes should then be shown to the Chairman who may amend them if they are defective in his/her view. The finalised version is then reproduced and circulated to the members of the Committee, where they will form the basis of the next meeting.

**20 How can you learn the skills needed for business meetings?**

The best way to learn is by taking an active part in meetings, either as chairman, secretary or simply by making a contribution to discussion. Do not shrink from taking responsibility. You are most likely to improve your command of the English language if you have to use English in the practical affairs of a business. You can prepare yourself for such a role by attending meetings whenever an opportunity occurs and observing the chairman, secretary and other officials and their conduct of the meeting.

**Written Exercise:** *Draw up an imaginary set of minutes for a Safety Committee meeting. Your minutes should include the following: (a) Name of committee, date, time and place of meeting. (b) List of those present, apologies for absence, minutes of the previous meeting agreed and signed by the Chairman as a true record. Matters arising – the Chairman attended the funeral of a wireman killed in an accident and reports on the welfare arrangements made. (c) Motions were moved about: (1) the provision of safety doors for fire precautions; (2) the setting up of a manual of procedures for electricians. A subcommittee was formed to write the manual. There was no other business.*

*Go over the topic again until you are sure of all the answers. Then tick it off on the check list at the back of the book.*

# 6 Business meetings – 2: terminology

**1 What does the word 'terminology' mean?**

It means 'specialised vocabulary' – the special words used in any particular activity – in this case when organising a meeting.

**2 What slang word do we use to describe specialist terminology?**

It is called jargon.

**3 Should we sneer at jargon?**

No – we should learn the specialised vocabulary.

**4 What is a quorum?**

The minimum number of members that must be present at a meeting under the rules, if the proceedings are to be valid.

**5 What does *ex officio* mean?**

'By virtue of office'. An official may automatically qualify for a position because of the office he/she holds. Thus a Personnel Officer may *ex officio* be a member of the Industrial Relations Committee of a company.

**6 What does the word 'co-opt' mean?**

Co-option is the power of a committee to ask others to serve on the committee if it seems that their expertise will be helpful. Usually a person may be co-opted by a simple majority vote of the committee.

**7 What is a 'motion'?**

A motion is a proposition for consideration at a meeting. It should normally be written out and handed to the chairman or secretary in advance, so that it can be included in the agenda – but as a matter of urgency a motion may be introduced at a meeting, if the meeting agrees.

**8 Who speaks to the motion?**

The **proposer**, who is followed by the **seconder**. A discussion then follows and the proposer has the right to reply to the discussion.

**9 What is an amendment?**

It is a suggestion to alter the wording of a motion during the course of discussion to make it more acceptable to the meeting, or cover some point omitted from the original motion. It must be proposed and seconded. If there is no seconder it is not proceeded with. If the amendment is carried, the motion is forthwith amended.

**10 What is a resolution?**

It is a formal decision carried at a meeting. It is proposed, seconded and carried – i.e. passed by a majority vote.

**11 In what ways may a resolution be carried?**

(a) Unanimously – everyone in agreement. (b) *Nem. con.* – no one contradicting. Some people voted in favour, and no one against, but some people did not vote. (c) By a majority – say 8 : 3 or 7 : 5. The majority required may be specified in the rules. (d) By the Chairman's casting vote – if voting is exactly equal, the Chairman may be allowed a second vote to resolve the difficulty, if this is allowed under the constitution of the club or organisation concerned.

**12 What does the phrase 'lie on the table' mean?**

It is used when no further action will be taken on a letter, document or motion at this particular meeting. The matter will then be given time for developments to take place, and may be raised at the next meeting if anyone is interested.

**13 What does a proposal that 'the meeting proceeds to the next business' mean?**

It means that the matter under discussion shall be left for the present – having been well and truly aired and no agreement seeming likely – and that the next item on the agenda should be discussed.

**14 What does the phrase 'proposed that the motion be now put' mean?**

It means that the discussion in the view of the proposer has gone on long enough and that the Chairman should put it to the vote. If this is carried, the proposer of the original motion is allowed to reply to the discussion and then the motion is voted upon.

**15 What are 'standing orders'?**

A body of rules, built up over the years or agreed to from the start of an organisation (in a constitution) which governs the procedure of the organisation's affairs, and particularly the conduct of meetings.

**16 What does 'On a point of order, Mr Chairman!' mean?**

It is a way of interrupting procedures if the rules of conduct are not being observed. Thus if a member is abusive, or calls another member a liar, or makes personal remarks about someone who is not present, or if the Chairman does not follow procedure, any member may stop procedings to draw the attention of the meeting to the breach of the rules. A common case is absence of a quorum – as when some members leave early.

**17 What is an 'adjournment'?**

It is the breaking-off of a meeting, to postpone further discussion or because time is short. The Chairman proposes an adjournment and if the meeting agrees, discussion will proceed at a later meeting, for which adequate notice will be given.

**Written Exercise:** *Draw up a short constitution for a drama society, tennis club or other recreational body, mentioning the rights and duties of members, the membership of the committee and the frequency and conduct of meetings.*

*Go over the topic again until you are sure of all the answers. Then tick it off on the check list at the back of the book.*

# 7 Listening and speaking at meetings

**1 What is the difference between passive and active listening?**

Passive listening occurs when someone is not concentrating on what is being said; he hears the words, but does not think about them. When a person is listening **attentively** and **critically, thinking** about what is being said, it is called **active listening**. Active listening is essential at business meetings.

## 2 How can you develop active listening?

(a) You must be able to *concentrate* on what is being said, listening closely for information which you require. One way to improve your concentration is to take notes, so that you have to listen for relevant details. (b) A good listener must develop a *sensitivity* to the speaker's voice. In speech a variation of tone, volume or pace, the use of stress or pauses, the choice of words, etc., will indicate to the listener ideas beyond the mere content of speech. (c) Be aware of the *structure* of a formal speech, noting when a speaker moves from his introduction to the development of his main ideas and on to a conclusion. (d) *Listen critically*. Think about what the speaker is saying, and decide for yourself whether or not you agree with him/her, and why.

## 3 What should you remember when speaking at a business meeting?

The points to remember may vary according to whether you are making a formal speech, giving a report or are involved in a discussion. However, there are some basic rules which should be followed.

(a) Speak clearly: make sure that your pronunciation can be understood. (b) Vary the tone of your speech. People who speak in a monotone soon lose the attention of their audiences. (c) Make sure that you can be heard by everyone at the meeting. You should not need to shout, but don't whisper either. (d) Try to maintain a measured pace. Do not speak too quickly, as your audience may not be able to follow you. Also, avoid a slow delivery which can quickly become tedious. In fact, a variety of pace is the best approach to public speaking. (e) Always remember the importance of the pause. After you have made an important point, pause briefly.

This is effective for two reasons; it gives the listeners an opportunity to take in what you have said, and it emphasises the importance of the statement, by drawing attention to it. (f) You should maintain eye-to-eye contact with your audience. Do not look vaguely into the distance, but focus on a member of the meeting at each point, and look him/her in the eye. (g) Remember who your audience is, and speak in an appropriate style. Use language that can be understood by the members. Do not try to impress by using difficult vocabulary or jargon when it is not appropriate. Do not speak down to the audience, but address them naturally, in a style that is neither too casual nor too formal.

**4 What should you remember when making a formal speech?**

Besides all the points mentioned in the previous answer, you should make sure that your speech is properly researched, carefully planned, as brief as possible, bearing in mind the points you have to make, and well rehearsed,

**5 Why does the speech need to be researched?**

In order to speak confidently, you must know as much as possible about the subject; in fact you should know more than is actually delivered in the speech. Try to predict possible questions which may be asked of you when you have finished speaking.

**6 How should a speech be planned?**

Like a written report, a formal speech needs to have a tight structure. The usual format is the introduction, followed by the body of the speech, in which you develop your main points and finally the conclusion.

**7 Why should a speech be short?**

Long, rambling speeches fail in the objective of communicating information to the audience, because people cannot maintain a high enough level of concentration. You should not introduce too many points into your speech (five to seven separate points is enough), and you should develop them clearly and succinctly. Avoid repetition of ideas, except in your brief summary in the conclusion.

**8 Why is it important to rehearse your speech?**

You need to fix the format of the speech in your mind. When rehearsing it, you must speak aloud, so that you can hear which parts of the speech you need to pay particular attention to. Also, you should be thinking about how you might vary volume, tone and pace, and where you should pause.

**9 How can you rehearse your speech?**

The best way is to practise your speech in front of a friend or colleague, who will be able to give constructive criticism on both content and the delivery. Also, you could record your speech, so that you can hear what it sounds like yourself.

**10 Should a formal speech be read or memorised verbatim?**

No. A speech which is read or memorised can either become dull or may be poorly presented because the speaker is concentrating on reading the text, rather than maintaining contact with his audience.

**11 What then is the best way to approach the presentation of a speech?**

You should make a set of brief notes covering the points you wish to raise in your speech. These notes act as a reminder, ensuring that you do not omit anything important. They should not be detailed, but should merely include key words and phrases which indicate the area you are going to speak about. It is a good idea to write your brief notes on postcards, one card per topic. But do remember to put the cards in the correct order. A treasury tag through a punched hole in the corner of each card keeps them in the correct order.

**12 What should you remember when taking part in a discussion?**

Many of the points made earlier concerning delivery, empathy with the audience, style, etc., apply here too. Try to ensure that what you are saying is relevant to the discussion. There is nothing more annoying in a meeting than to have someone introducing a subject which is off the point. Also you should have an idea of what you are going to say before you begin, otherwise your contribution may become halting, repetitive or irrelevant.

**Written Exercise: *Prepare a formal speech on the following topic:***

**The impact of microtechnology in the office**

*Using brief notes make the speech to a friend and/or record it. Afterwards, analyse critically the organisation and delivery of your speech.*

*Go over the topic again until you are sure of all the answers. Then tick it off on the check list at the back of the book.*

# 8 The style and tone of business English

**1 What is meant by *style* in written English?**

*Style* means the type of language we use to convey our thoughts or information. For example the style of a poem will be very different from the style of a scientific report.

**2 What determines the style of our writing?**

Writing style will vary, depending on the reasons for writing, the type of audience and the material you wish to communicate.

**3 How can you vary style?**

Style is varied by using a different vocabulary, by altering sentence structure, sentence organisation, voice and register.

**4 What should be the style of business writing?**

Business correspondence is a permanent, tangible record of a business relationship. It is vital that any communication is unambiguous. Therefore, all business writing should be in a clear style, so that the reader has no difficulty in understanding the content. Any confusion caused by a poorly written letter, or a report which does not communicate its contents effectively, may disrupt business activity.

**5 How do you achieve a clear style?**

The vocabulary used should be appropriate for the reader. Long and difficult words should be avoided if simpler vocabulary can be used. Sentences should not be too lengthy with many subordinate clauses. A variety of sentence structures prevents the material from becoming dull.

**6 What do we mean by the tone or register of a communication?**

By tone or register, we mean the way a speaker or writer addresses his audience. For example, a letter written to a close friend will be casual in tone, personal and colloquial. On the other hand, a letter to a bank manager asking for an overdraft will be formal and less personal.

**7 What should be the tone of business communication?**

Once again, this will vary according to the type of communication, and its intended audience. Courtesy is essential in business correspondence, as it promotes the goodwill necessary between business houses. Generally business letters should not be impersonal; neither should they be too casual in tone.

**8 What should be the tone of a written report?**

Reports are usually impersonal and formal in tone. The writer may use the passive voice, so that the emphasis is on the activities which have been carried out, rather than the people who performed those activities. This is especially true of scientific reports.

**9 Why is it important to bear in mind the person who will read the business communication?**

It is necessary, so that the right style and tone are chosen. You must alter the vocabulary you use, and the sentence structure so that you can communicate clearly to your audience. A technical report to be circulated to a group of researchers will probably use scientific language or jargon. On the other hand, a general letter distributed to shopfloor workers will be written in a different style, so that it is more easily read.

**10 What is *ambiguity*?**

Ambiguity is a 'double-meaning' in a sentence, which leaves the reader or listener unsure about what is actually meant. For example, in the following sentence, it is not clear whether the adverb *rarely* modifies the verb *repair* or the verb *get rich*.

*People who repair machines rarely get rich.*

Similarly the following sentence is ambiguous because it is not clear whether it is the foreman or the manager who was taken ill.

*When the foreman arrived at the manager's office he was taken ill.*

**11 What do we mean by *obscurity*?**

Obscurity occurs when a sentence is so badly organised or expressed that its meaning is not clear. Even more serious than an obscure sentence is a longer piece of writing which is so confused that it is not possible to understand what the passage as a whole is trying to tell us.

**12 How can you avoid ambiguity or obscurity?**

You must put yourself in the place of the reader and ask yourself whether you would understand what the writer was trying to communicate if you had no prior knowledge of the subject. If the communication is at all unclear, then rewriting is necessary. You should always read through any letter or report after you have written it to check for clarity and precision of expression.

**13 When is a paragraph finished?**

It is not finished when you stop writing it. It is finished when you have read it through and approved it for clarity and style.

**14 What is *slang*?**

Slang words and phrases are expressions in common, colloquial use, but considered outside the general body of standard English, and therefore inappropriate for formal communication. For example, the verb *to diddle* is slang for *to cheat*, but it should not be used in business correspondence. We would not say:

*Take care that you are not diddled by the freight agents.*

**15 Why should clichés be avoided?**

A cliché is a word or phrase which has been so over-used that it has lost its original meaning. You should avoid such outworn phrases in business correspondence as they do not communicate accurately.

**16 What is wrong with some phrases used in business?**

In the past, businesses have developed forms of commercial English which have been so over-used that they have become clichés, verbose and even meaningless. For example, the phrase

*We beg to acknowledge receipt of your letter* could simply be written as *Thank you for your letter.*

**Written Exercise: *Rewrite the following sentences in more direct English, avoiding so far as possible, the words in bold type.***
*(a)* **Further to our letter of yesterday's date** *we can now confirm the dispatch of the goods by surface freight.* *(b)* **As your agents in East Africa it is incumbent upon us to** *explain the loss of the goods.* *(c)* **It is our honest belief that** *the documentation you supplied was inaccurate and misleading.* *(d)* **I beg to offer my poor services** *as secretary to your managing director.* *(e)* **It will be our earnest endeavour** *to meet your requirements* **in every particular.**

*Go over the topic again until you are sure of all the answers. Then tick it off on the check list at the back of the book.*

# 9 Form design for business use

**1 What is the advantage of using forms in business?**

They make a routine procedure out of a specialist activity. For example, we no longer need to write a letter to place an order with a supplier – we use a specialist order form. By filling in the little boxes saying the number required of each listed item we can place an accurate order more quickly then by writing a letter.

**2 Why is a knowledge of English essential for form design?**

Forms must be clear and unambiguous. They must be expressed in simple language so that even the least sophisticated people can complete them properly. They must elicit every piece of information required.

**3 What is a basic consideration when drawing up a form?**

Is there any international or national standard to conform with? For example, in international trade, a United Nations

Committee has agreed a layout which will be followed by all nations for the import and export trades.

**4 What is the basis of this format?**

(a) It is based on A4 paper. (b) The surface area of the paper is divided into areas called 'fields'. Each field has been allocated to a particular piece of information – for example Exporter, Consignee, Name of Vessel, Port of Departure, Port of Arrival, etc., etc.

**5 Supposing you do not stick to the format – what happens?**

(a) At worst your goods are sent off to the wrong destination, or (b) at best they are subject to delay. Imagine – the goods arrive in a foreign port. The customs officer has a limited command of English. He looks in the box for the Consignee's name. However it reads 2700 kilograms – you have put the wrong information in the box. He leaves your goods until last, and deals with goods where the forms are correctly completed.

**6 What other considerations are basic to form design?**

A form usually has legal implications. It may make a binding contract between seller and buyer, or it may be used in an insurance claim. We must make sure that if there are legal implications we meet the requirements fully.

**7 When designing a form what are the rules about the wording?**

(a) As little wording as possible. (b) A space wherever an answer is required. (c) Give your own name and address clearly if the form is to be returned to you.

**8 Consider the form in Fig. 9.1. What is the correct way to indicate which item you require?**

We could put a tick in the box. However, most typewriter keyboards do not have a 'tick', so it is usual to put an x in the box – a small letter x if such a form is completed by a typist.

## Household Supplies (Wholesale) Ltd

4145 Camside, Cambridge, CB4 1PQ

☐ Your new catalogue please
☐ Literature on garage accessories please

Name_____

Company_____

Address_____

_____

_____

_____ Postcode_____

**Note:** Orders based on the brochures can
only be supplied to retailers – no orders
from householders please.

Fig. 9.1 A simple order form from a
trade magazine

**9 In designing an order form, what does the seller bear in mind?**

(a) The order represents a contract between the parties, so it must have the names and addresses of both firms. (b) The goods are listed in a convenient sequence for order picking. The order picking lift truck comes to the goods in a certain order in the warehouse and the goods are listed in that order. (c) The names, sizes and codings are printed for each item. (d) There is a space for the customer to insert the number required. (e) The order may have several copies for use by various departments – warehouse, despatch, delivery note with space for customer's signature, etc.

**10** Look at the order form in Fig. 9.2. It is used for taking telephone orders of perishable milk products. What does ASAP mean?

As soon as possible.

**11** Explain the phrase 'Terms nett payable 30 days from actual delivery date'

It means the full charge (no discount given) is payable in 30 days, counting from the date of delivery – not the date the order was placed.

**Written Exercise 1:** *Your firm publishes a 'free circulation' magazine called Jobseek which is sent out monthly to all personnel officers or others interested in finding staff. You want to increase the circulation but only to genuine staff in personnel departments. Design a form allowing readers to request that their names be added to the mailing list but enabling you to send a letter of regret if they are clearly unsuitable.*

**Written Exercise 2:** *Your firm is doing a piece of market research for the Spanish Government. They want to know what people who travelled to Spain for a holiday this year thought of: (a) the resort they visited, (b) the beaches, (c) the hotels, (d) the food, (e) their personal safety. They would also like to know: (a) how much they paid for the holiday, (b) how much they spent as pocket money, (c) whether they hired a car or a moped, (d) how much they spent on souvenirs. Design a form to elicit this information (and any other you feel is relevant). Give them at least one chance to write freely about anything they feel is important.*

*Go over the topic again until you are sure of all the answers. Then tick it off on the check list at the back of the book.*

# 10 Questionnaires for market research

**1 What is a questionnaire?**

It is a set of written questions designed to discover public opinion on a particular point, or public need in a particular area.

**DELIVERY NOTE NO.** 13301

# BAILEY MILK PRODUCTS LTD

29 BRIGHTON ROAD · CRAWLEY · WEST SUSSEX · RH10 6AE
Tel: CRAWLEY (0293) 511311 · Telex: 87464 · Regd. No. 1524937 England

| INVOICE TO: | DELIVER TO: |
|---|---|
| Speedy Dairies Ltd<br>Old Mill Road<br>Cambridge<br>CB2 1SQ | The Wellcome Dairy<br>2174 Camside<br>Chesterton<br>Cambridge<br>CB4 1PQ |

| ACCOUNT NUMBER<br>01 4892 _ _ _ | BRANCH NUMBER<br>4 | CUSTOMER ORDER No.<br>D 1037 | ORDER DATE<br>11.12.-- | CUSTOMER CATEGORY<br>C |
|---|---|---|---|---|

| CODE | PRODUCT DESCRIPTION | QUANTITY PER TRAY | NO. OF TRAYS ORDERED | NO. OF TRAYS RECEIVED | REMARKS |
|---|---|---|---|---|---|
| Y01- | 'Frutti' Yogurt Multi-pack Cherry/Strawberry | 6 x 4 x 125g | 180 | | |
| Y02- | 'Frutti' Yogurt Multi-pack Apple/Orange Cherry/Orange | 6 x 4 x 125g | 180 | | |
| Y03- | 'Frutti' Yogurt Multi-pack Cherry/Strawberry/ Apricot | 8 x 3 x 125g | | | |
| Y04- | | | | | |
| Y05- | 'Fruit Basket' Yogurt Kiwi/Gooseberry Apricot/Mango | 20 x 150g | | | |
| Y06- | 'Fruit Basket' Yogurt Morello Cherry/Elderberry Plum/Walnut | 20 x 150g | | | |
| Y07- | Fruit Yogurt Cherry 500g | 12 x 500g | | | |
| Y08- | Fruit Yogurt Strawberry 500g | 12 x 500g | | | |
| Y09- | Fruit Yogurt Apricot 500g | 12 x 500g | | | |
| Y10- | Fruit Yogurt Mixed Fruit 500g | 12 x 500g | | | |
| Y11- | 'Frutti' Yogurt 150g pots Cherry/Strawberry | 20 x 150g | | | |
| Y12- | | | | | |
| Y13- | | | | | |
| Y14- | | | | | |
| D01- | 'Puddi' Chocolate Dessert | 12 x 2 x 125g | 90 | | |
| D02- | | | | | |
| D03- | Chocolate Dessert with Cream | 20 x 125g | | | |
| M01- | 'Drink Me' Banana Milk Drink | 24 x 200ml | | | |
| M02- | 'Drink Me' Strawberry Milk Drink | 24 x 200ml | | | |
| M03- | 'Drink Me' Chocolate Milk Drink | 24 x 200ml | | | |
| M04- | | | | | |
| C01- | U.H.T. Whipping Cream 35% Fat | 24 x 200ml | | | |
| C02- | | | | | |
| C03- | | | | | |
| | | **TOTAL TRAYS** | 450 | | |

| SPECIAL DELIVERY INSTRUCTIONS<br>ASAP and no later than 17.12.-- | RECEIVED VIA:<br>LOWFIELD DISTRIBUTION LTD.<br><br>TERMS:<br>NETT PAYABLE 30 DAYS FROM ACTUAL DELIVERY DATE | CUSTOMER SIGNATURE OR P.O.D. STAMP<br><br><br>DATE DELIVERED:............................................ |
|---|---|---|

**Fig. 9.2 A more sophisticated order form**

## 2 How is it used?

It is sent to a representative sample of those interested (or a sample of the public at large). They complete the questionnaire and return it to the researchers, who record the responses and analyse them, producing a report on the results.

## 3 What are the advantages of inquiries by written questionnaires?

(a) They reach the right people to respond – they are put into the in-trays of the person most likely to deal with them (for example, a transport questionnaire would go to the transport manager). (b) They can be carefully thought out and cover the subject of the enquiry comprehensively. (c) The cost is low, and expensive interviewers need not be employed. (d) The repondent doesn't have to give answers on the spur of the moment but may consult records, etc. (e) Responses do not all arrive at the same time and can be dealt with in turn as received.

## 4 What are the problems when designing a written questionnaire?

We must:
(a) Keep the instructions clear and simple, and as short as possible. (b) Make it clear who should answer it – for preference – e.g. the transport manager. (c) If the completion of the form is compulsory make this clear and tell the reader what the penalty is for non-compliance. (d) If it is voluntary, solicit the cooperation of the respondent and stress the non-personal nature of the inquiry and the preservation of privacy, if this is likely to be important. (e) Keep each question short – answerable by ticking yes/no boxes if possible. (f) If this is not possible limit the answer – i.e. was it excellent, good, fair, poor or bad (tick the correct answer)? (g) Give clear instructions about the

# Department of Tourism Magalufia

As you leave Magalufia today would you please complete the enclosed form (by ticking the appropriate boxes) and give it to the departure lounge hostess before departure. We hope this survey will improve our service to tourists.

Thank you for your co-operation.

| | |
|---|---|
| 1 | **How long did you stay in Magalufia?**<br>7 days or less ☐　　8–15 days ☐　　More than 15 days ☐ |
| 2 | **Where did you stay?**　　Hotel ☐　　Self-catering apartment ☐<br>Small lodging house ☐　　With friends ☐ |
| 3 | **How much did you spend altogether on accommodation?**<br>less than £100 ☐　　£100–£199 ☐　　£200 or more ☐ |
| 4 | **How much spending money did you spend altogether while you were here?**　　less than £100 ☐　　£100–£199 ☐<br>£200–£299 ☐　　£300 or more ☐ |
| 5 | **During your stay did you engage in any of the following activities?**<br>sailing ☐　　tennis ☐<br>wind-surfing ☐　　driving ☐<br>water-skiing ☐　　moped touring ☐<br>parascending ☐　　sea fishing ☐ |
| 6 | **Did you visit any of the following attractions?**<br>Magalufia Zoo ☐　　The Casino ☐<br>Magalufia Dolphinarium ☐　　The Esperanza Disco ☐<br>The caves of Fumentoza ☐　　The Royal Ballet ☐<br>The mountains of Hortenza ☐　　The Equestrian School ☐ |
| 7 | Would you please name any facility we do not have which would add to the pleasure of a future holiday.<br><br>_____ |

Thank you for your help. Do come again next year.

**Fig. 10.1 A simple questionnaire**

return of the questionnaire, the name and address, postcode, etc.

**5 What English qualities are helpful in designing a questionnaire?**

(a) A clear and simple style. (b) A wide vocabulary – we can usually be brief if we know exactly the right word to use in any particular situation. (c) A logical order is essential so that the sequence of questions leads on to investigate the subject area as exhaustively as possible, without becoming a bore.
A typical questionnare is illustrated in Fig. 10.1.

**Written Exercise 1:** *Design a questionnaire to be used in your school or college to discover what types of transport are used by students to reach the premises, how much each student spends on travel per week and what proportion this is of their total income from all sources.*

**Written Exercise 2:** *Design a questionnaire to be used to keep a record of accidents in a small factory. The forms will be sent to Head Office to acquaint them with all the particulars of each accident, date, time, nature of the occurrence, who was involved, who treated the injured person, etc. A space for the signature of the supervisor concerned should be provided.*

*Go over the topic again until you are sure of all the answers. Then tick it off on the check list at the back of the book.*

# 11 Telex messages

**1 What is the telex system?**

A system for sending messages nationally and internationally over telegraph lines from one subscriber to another. Connections are made by automatic exchanges similar to telephone exchanges.

**2 How does the system work?**

Every subscriber has a telex number or code which is listed in a telex directory. To call a subscriber you type this code on your telex machine. If the subscriber's machine is available (not busy with another message) it send its answer-back code to show it is ready. You then transmit your message and at the end repeat the call code. It replies with its answer back code, thus proving that the whole message has been received. A copy of the message appears on both sender's and receiver's machine.

**3 What are the advantages of the system?**

(a) It is instantaneous – the message arrives at the other side of the world in seconds. (b) It ignores time scales – a message from UK in daytime arrives in Australia in the middle of the night. Next morning the Australian telex operator tears off the overnight messages and passes them to the person named on the attention line. (c) No one can stop a telex – if you are trying to reach the top man/woman in an organisation send him/her a telex.

**4 What is the defect of the telex?**

Since personal signatures cannot be sent it is debatable whether a telex can in fact make a binding contract between the parties. It is safest to confirm them by airmail letter if they are intended to form a contract.

**5 What is the style of a telex message?**

It is factual, clear and avoids the niceties of conversational English. It also avoids wordy sentences, clichés and redundant expressions. It abbreviates sentences by leaving out the definite and indefinite articles, conjunctions, pronouns, etc., and it abbreviates common words.

**6 Give examples of common abbreviations**

| | | |
|---:|:---:|:---|
| TLX | = | telex |
| OTLX | = | our telex |
| YTLX | = | your telex |
| YR | = | your |
| ATTN | = | attention |

Any technical word that will be
understood at the other end can be
abbreviated – just as a secretary
develops his/her own short forms:
x = express, GAR = garments,
IT = information technology.
An imaginary telex message is shown in
Fig. 11.1 (Note: IMM = immediately).

```
86-01-23      10:30
OUR REF: 4712/GW    86-01-23    10:30
276134    SURFA G
57012     INSUR I

ATTN  SIG BARBIROLLI

PLEASE SURVEY IMM MV SAN ANGELO NAPLES SUSPICION ARSON TLX
OPINION EARLIEST POSSIBLE AIRMAIL CONFIRMATION FOLLOWS

REGARDS

GREYSTOKE MARINE INSURANCE

276134    SURFA G
57012     INSUR I
```

**Fig. 11.1  An imaginary telex
message (No similarity to any telex
subscriber or ship intended).**

**Written Exercise:** *John Todd of Lionheart Productions, whose telex code
is 147568 and answer back code is LIONP G wishes to contact Golden
Oldie Films, whose telex code is 385241 and answerback code is GOLDO
S. He wants a retired film star Max Offero to play a small part in a London
based production starting on 25th September. Draw up the telex to Golden
Oldie's manager Helen Fullbright.*

*Go over the topic again until you are sure of all the answers. Then tick it
off on the check list at the back of the book.*

# 12 Applying for employment

**1 How should you apply for an office post?**

This may vary, according to the type of job you are applying for and the demands of the employer. The most common way is to apply formally by letter, but some firms conduct **walk-in interviews**, when an applicant merely turns up at an office or factory and has an interview immediately. In some cases, application for a job requires the completion of an application form. In this unit, we shall only consider application by letter.

**2 Where can you find out about available jobs?**

(a) Most vacancies are advertised in the local or national press. If you see a job you would like in the newspaper, you will probably have to write a letter to the employers, or phone them to arrange an interview. (b) Your country may have **employment offices**. These may be public or private organisations which bring the employer and the job-hunter together. A firm which needs new employees informs the employment office of its requirements, and the office will contact appropriate workers. If they are interested in applying for the vacancies, the employment office will probably arrange an interview for them with the firm. (c) Many firms advertise vacancies outside their offices and factories on large notice-boards. (d) It is possible to find out about vacancies by talking to people who are already at work. They may have inside knowledge of people who have recently left, or who intend to leave their jobs.

**3 How should a letter of application be set out?**

Your letter should be set out formally, as suggested in *Unit 15, English I: Writing*

*Business Letters*. That is, it should include:
(a) your address in the top right-hand corner; (b) lower down, on the left hand side, the address of the person to whom you are writing; (c) the date you are writing the letter; (d) any references; (e) the salutation (Dear Sir, Dear Madam, etc.); (f) a subject heading; (g) a brief introductory paragraph; (h) main paragraphs; (i) a concluding paragraph; (j) the complimentary close; (k) your signature.

**4 To whom should you write the letter?**

The name of the person will probably be given in the advertisement. If no name is given, then address your letter to 'The Personnel Manager', if you are applying to a large organisation, or 'The Manager' if the business is small.

**5 What should be included in the subject heading?**

As you already know, the subject heading states the main content of your letter. Therefore, it will probably be something like:

*Application for post of General Clerk*

Remember that your subject heading should be underlined.

**6 What should you mention in the introductory paragraph?**

You should briefly refer to the job you are applying for, and where you saw it advertised. For example:

*I wish to apply for the above-mentioned post, advertised in the* Chesterbridge Chronicle *on 23rd August 19...*

**7 How many main paragraphs should you write?**

This will depend on two main factors. Firstly the amount of experience you have. Secondly the type of job you are applying for. If you are a school leaver, with little experience, you will probably only need to write one main paragraph.

However, if you are older, and have had several jobs or taken relevant courses, etc., you may wish to include all this information in separate main paragraphs.

**8 What is the most important thing to remember about the information in these paragraphs?**

All the information included must be *brief* and must be *relevant*. Prospective employers will not be interested in details about your life which do not relate directly to the job for which you are applying.

For example, suppose you included the information that you represented your school in the national swimming championships. Such detail would be appropriate if you were applying for the post of trainee lifeguard at the local swimming pool, but would be totally irrelevant if you were seeking a job as a librarian's assistant.

**9 What details should be included in the main paragraphs?**

(a) You should refer to your educational achievements, listing examinations you have passed, courses attended, etc. It is also appropriate to mention any experience you have had which will enhance your chances of being given the post. For example, if you are applying for a job as trainee sales manager with a large department store, and you have worked part-time as a weekend shop assistant while you attended school, it would be relevant to mention that experience. (b) You may be required to submit the name (or names) of one or more people who can give you a **reference**.

**10 What is a reference?**

A reference is a statement, made by someone who knows you well, about your qualities. Normally, it will refer to things like your punctuality, attitude towards work, reliability, relationship with others, etc. The reference will be sent to a prospective employer so that he/she has some idea of the sort of person you are before interviewing you.

**11 Who should you choose as a referee**

Quite often you have no choice. The prospective employer will probably insist that the referee be either your former headmaster or college principal or your last employer. If you are free to nominate your own referee, choose someone you can rely on, who is able to write clearly and give a fair report on you. Avoid anyone who will just write a reference overflowing with praise for you; it is likely to make a prospective employer suspicious about the referee's impartiality.

**12 What is included in the last paragraph?**

The last paragraph gives you an opportunity to express your willingness to attend an interview, and to meet any conditions laid down in the advertisement. For example, if the job demands that you work night shifts, you should state that you are prepared to do this.

**13 What form should the complimentary close take?**

As the letter is formal, it should close with *Yours sincerely* or *Yours faithfully*, depending on whether you know the name of the person to whom you are writing or not.

**14 How should the letter be presented?**

It is important to remember that the presentation of your letter will create an immediate impression on the reader. A letter which is neatly written and clearly set out will stand more chance of a second reading than an untidily presented letter. If you are applying for many jobs, avoid giving the impression that your letter has been duplicated, and that you are merely sending out copies to different employers.

**15 What should be the tone of the letter?**

It is a formal letter, but it should not be too cold or impersonal. Also, you should remember to be polite. Try to convey a feeling of enthusiasm for the job, without sounding over-zealous.

**Written Exercise 1:** *Read the following letter of application, and then write the advertisement to which it is a response.*

The Personnel Manager,
South Sea Oil Ltd,
Jurong Road,
Seatown,
Sussex, BN15 4FR

36, Whitman Road,
Sussex Estate,
Lower Heath,
Essex, CM14 7JU
15th July 19. .

Dear Sir,

*Application for post as Trainee Turner*

I would like to apply for the above post, advertised in the *Seatown News* on 14th July 19...

I am a seventeen year old student, presently attending a course in lathe engineering at Lower Heath Technical College. Last year I left Lower Heath Comprehensive School, having gained five 'O' level passes in English, Mathematics, Technical Drawing, Metalwork and Physics. While at school I was a member of the Creative Metalwork Club.

My course at the technical college began in September 19. . and will be completed at the end of this month. During the year I have worked on various lathes and other types of metal-cutting machinery. My lecturer on the course, Mr John Williams, has agreed to give me a reference, should you require one.

In the advertisement, you mention that the successful applicant would be expected to attend a day-release course at the technical college. I would welcome such an opportunity to improve my skills.

I would be grateful if you could offer me an interview at any time.

Yours faithfully
Martin Wright

**Written Exercise 2:** *Write a letter of application in response to the following job advertisement.*

**SITUATION VACANT**

We are a wholesale trading firm specialising in the supply of farm machinery, fertilisers, weedkillers, insecticides, etc. We require several trainee sales persons. Candidates should have at least 3 'O' Level passes, including English and Maths. Some experience or knowledge of farming is essential.

The successful candidate will be expected to attend day release and evening courses at Seatown Polytechnic.

Interested candidates should apply to:

**The Personnel Manager**
**Farm Suppliers Ltd**
**Warehouse No. 4**
**Seatown Industrial Estate**
**Seatown**
**Sussex**
**SU3 PR7**

*The names and addresses of two referees should be submitted.*

*Go over the topic again until you are sure of all the answers. Then tick it off on the check list at the back of the book.*


# 13 Interviews

**1 How should a candidate prepare for an interview?**

Although it is difficult to predict everything you will be asked at an interview, you should think about the questions you may be asked, and consider how you will answer them. Try to put yourself in the place of the interviewer and imagine what he is looking for in the interviewee. Your aim is to convince the interviewer that you can meet his/her requirements in every respect. Try to envisage what those requirements could be.

**2 Is your appearance important when attending an interview?**

Yes. No matter how unimportant you may think it is, your appearance will definitely have an effect on the interviewer. You should look clean and tidy.

**3 How should you conduct yourself in an interview?**

(a) Try to be as relaxed as possible. It is natural to be nervous during an interview, but try to control your nerves; do not fidget. On the other hand, you must not be so relaxed as to be casual in your attitude. (b) Be polite: do not sit down until you are invited to do so, and thank the interviewer when the interview is over. Address the interviewer courteously.

**4 What should you remember when speaking during an interview?**

(a) Speak clearly: do not rush your answers or speak so quietly that you can barely be heard. (b) Look at the interviewer; eye-to-eye contact is important in establishing a rapport between yourself and the person to whom you are speaking. Do not look vaguely round the room or stare out of the window.

**5 What should you do if you cannot answer a question?**

Be honest, and admit that you do not know the answer. If you try to reply when you do not know what you are talking about, the interviewer will soon detect your ignorance.

**6 What should you remember when answering questions?**

Make sure that your answer is relevant. Keep to the point, and do not ramble on to a different subject. Avoid repeating yourself. Your answer should be as full as possible. You should not normally give brief, one word answers.

**7 Should you ask questions?**

Yes, if you are given the opportunity to do so. It is a good idea to prepare some questions in advance which will show the interviewer that you are taking an intelligent interest in the job, and with a view to long-term employment. For example 'I would like to know what long-term prospects there are in this position. Is there a chance for me in the future to progress to higher grades of employment?' Or perhaps 'If I enter this branch of the industry, is there a professional body of which I should aim to achieve membership?'

There may be important points you want to raise with the interviewer, and details you need to confirm, but do not give the impression that you have serious reservations about the job.

**8 Suppose you are the person conducting the interview. What should you do before it starts?**

(a) Consider what sort of a person is required to do the job effectively. Bear in mind the demands the job will make on the successful candidate. (b) Try to find out as much as possible about the applicant. Ask for references or testimonials well before the interview, so that you can study them before the interview takes place. (c) Prepare a series of questions to ask the candidate which will help to discover whether he/she is suitable for the post. (d) If a panel of interviewers is to be present decide which subject areas each will cover in questioning the candidates.

**9 What do you want your questions to reveal about the applicant?**

There are a number of points an interviewer is interested in: (a) Are the candidate's education and experience suitable for the job? (b) Does he/she have the right physique for the post? (c) Does he/she have the right character for the post? (d) Are his/her appearance, manner and speech acceptable? (e) Would he/she be able to work with others? (f) Would he/she accept advice willingly? (g) Is he/she interested in developing the necessary skills, taking on greater responsibilities and advancing to more senior positions? (h)

Does he/she seem to be an active person, with wide interests?
There are many other areas to be considered, which will vary according to the demands of the job.

**10 How should the interviewer relate to the candidate?**

People attending an interview are usually nervous. A good interviewer will try to put the candidate at ease. Do not be casual in your approach, as this might mislead the candidate, but do not be too formal or impersonal either.

**11 Why should you make the interviewee relax?**

If you are to find out as much as you can about the candidate, you need to develop a rapport with him/her. The candidate needs to feel relaxed enough so that he/she can speak freely and easily.

**12 How can you help the applicant feel more relaxed during the interview?**

Take a personal interest in the candidate. Ask your questions in a friendly, not intimidating, tone. Start with easy questions (so that the candidate can get used to the room, the interviewing panel, and the situation) before moving onto more demanding questions.

**13 How do you bring the interview to a close?**

When you feel you have found out as much about the candidate as you can, give him/her the opportunity to ask questions. This will reveal the depth of his/her interest in the job, and the extent to which he/she has thought intelligently about it.

**14 When should you make a decision on the choice of applicants?**

Do not make a decision until you have as much material as possible on each of the candidates. This includes references, testimonials and other reports.

**Practical Exercise:** *With a suitable partner, practise interviewing by rôle play. Obtain typical newspaper advertisements for job specifications, e.g. types of employment, conditions, etc. Then one person can interview the other, or a panel of interviewers can be formed to interview several applicants. Critically appraise each candidate. Did he/she interview well or poorly? How could their performances have been improved?*

*Go over the topic again until you are sure of all the answers. Then tick it off on the check list at the back of the book.*

# 14 The importance of reading

**1 Why is reading important?**

It depends on what you read, but the advantages of reading are that: (a) it helps you to broaden your knowledge of the world; (b) you can keep in touch with developments in your own particular field; (c) your command of English will improve; (d) it is a useful form of relaxation and source of pleasure; (e) it is the basis of communication in business. We receive memos, telexes, letters and reports from all parts of the world and take action upon them to promote our personal, and also the general, prosperity.

**2 What should you read to broaden your knowledge of the world?**

Any business person needs to keep in touch with social, cultural, economic and political developments all over the world. You should make a point of reading a good daily newspaper if one is available in your country.

**3 What is a *good* newspaper?**

It is a paper which is informative and well written. It should include an international news section, as well as national news, and reports or articles from specialist reporters. Read a paper which is *balanced* in its reports or editorials; that is, it presents facts in an objective way, giving different points of view on a subject. But we must also learn to 'read between the lines'.

**4 What does 'read between the lines' mean?**

It means many things. First of all a reporter who is in a difficult situation in a country where he is not free to tell the whole truth may seek to convey what is the true position in a veiled way, and we should be alert to detect any subtle indications of what the true situation is. Second, we should get to know the political and social stance of the various journals and take this bias into account in evaluating the opinions expressed.

**5 What else can you read besides newspapers if you wish to be well informed?**

There are many news magazines and periodicals available which provide useful reviews of recent events. Magazines such as *Time, Life, Newsweek, South, The Economist, The National Geographic Magazine, New Society*, etc., are available throughout much of the world.

**6 Why do you need to keep in touch with developments in your own particular field?**

An efficient business person must be aware of the latest developments in his specialist area, if he is not to fall behind his competitors. There are numerous trade and business journals covering many diverse aspects of industrial development, banking, finance, insurance, engineering, etc. These are often produced by national and international associations whose task it is to promote greater understanding of their particular area of concern among their members. It would probably be worth your while to subscribe to appropriate journals, particularly your own professional journal (for example the journal *Freight Forwarding* for the Freight Forwarders, or the *Insurance Brokers' Monthly* for those engaged in the insurance industry). There are also manuals of more general interest, such as Croner's reference books, for example the *Reference Book for Importers*, the *Reference Book for Exporters*, the *Reference Book for Employers*, etc.

**7 How does reading help to improve your command of English?**

In six chief ways. By improving (a) your vocabulary, (b) your knowledge of syntax, (c) your knowledge of sentence structure, (d) your ability to develop longer passages, (e) the subtlety of expression that is possible in English, (f) your general comprehension.

**8 How does reading help vocabulary?**

Your vocabulary will expand rapidly if you make a conscious effort to write down and learn new words you come across in your reading. In *Revise and Test Business English 1*, Topic 7, it was suggested that you buy a small notebook, enter in it any new word and its meaning, and learn the spelling and definition of the word. This activity need not take more than ten minutes a day, but your vocabulary should increase dramatically.

**9 What is syntax?**

It is the grammatical arrangement of words in a sentence. By regular reading you will unconsciously absorb English phrases and syntax which will help to make your own written and spoken expressions more fluent.

**10 How does reading help in writing longer passages such as essays and reports?**

It helps you to appreciate how a longer passage of writing is constructed; that is, how the writer develops and links his ideas. You will begin to appreciate the importance of the correct choice of a word to convey a fine shade of meaning. Through this, you will begin to understand the *attitude* of the writer towards his subject, and towards you, the reader. This will help you develop a style of your own which will bring a long report to life.

**11 Is reading for relaxation and pleasure justified for the modern businessman?**

Yes. Although people in business are very busy, it is essential that they forget their job at times; such a break ensures that they return to their task refreshed.

**12 What should you read?**

This depends entirely on your likes and interests. Choose books that you want to read and which are appropriate for your standard of English.

**13 How often should you read?**

Try to set aside some time each day to read. Make use of any space time, such as travelling to work by bus or train, for reading.

**14 What makes a good reader?**

A good reader should read *critically*, that is he must be thinking about what he is reading. He must have in mind his purposes for reading before he begins; for example, is he looking for specific information in a report, is he skimming through a passage to get a general outline of its content, is he reading for pleasure etc. *Concentration* is an important skill for a reader to develop. Also, a good reader must be able to comprehend the text; selecting relevant points; drawing inferences from the text and making general conclusions about the meaning of the passage. Finally, you must vary your approach when reading, adapting your style so that it is appropriate for your objectives and the types of material you are studying.

**Practical Exercise:** *Consider the field of business you are already in, or the most likely field you will enter when you leave school or college. Attempt to discover (a) the name of the journal published by the professional body concerned, (b) the name of a popular magazine or trade* *journal for the industry concerned, (c) using a good general library which has the index to the 'Economist' find 5 important articles about the industry in the last four years, and look up these articles.*

(Note: The Writers and Artists Year Book may help you with the names of magazines and journals. You will find a copy in most reference libraries.)

*Go over the topic again until you are sure of all the answers. Then tick it off on the check list at the back of the book.*

# 15 Organising a business correspondence department

**1 What is the problem in organising a business correspondence department?**

We have a large number of people initiating correspondence (the authors) and sending it to its appropriate destination (the addressees). In between them we have someone who actually types the letters, telexes, etc. We will call this person the 'word processor'. The problem is to ensure that every 'author' is provided economically with the services of an efficient 'word-processor'.

**2 In conducting a review of business correspondence services, what are the stages in the inquiry?**

(a) Discover who the authors are and what types of communications they are likely to initiate. (b) Discover what types of 'addressee' are involved, whether they are internal or external, and which types of correspondence are likely to produce the best responses from them. (c) Find what types of equipment are needed to produce the necessary memos, letters and reports. (d) Find what numbers of 'word processing' staff we require to produce the necessary memos, letters and reports, and what skills they should ideally have.

| | |
|---|---|
| **3 How could we conduct such a review of business correspondence?** | By asking everyone during a prescribed investigation period (say one or two weeks) to take an extra copy of each piece of work done. These extra copies would then be analysed and appraised for suitability and efficiency. Figure 15.1 shows a memo to staff requesting such a procedure. |
| **4 What will be the result of the investigation?** | Recommendations about reorganisation, technology and personnel. Any type of reorganisation involves expense in buying new equipment, retraining staff, rewriting manuals of procedures, etc. |
| **5 List some of the elements in any reorganisation** | (a) Specification of a house style for correspondence. (b) Training of management staff and supervisory staff in the writing of business letters. Often the 'authors' are less well educated in business English than their secretaries. All sorts of people become managers – technical staff, scientists, sales personnel. It doesn't mean they can write a good letter. (c) Training management and supervisors in dictation techniques. (d) Developing a training structure for all 'word processor' personnel to advance them within the firm to the point where they can do a range of jobs efficiently. Labour-turnover is a heavy business cost. The best policy is to train your own staff – if anyone does leave you always have a few people who are due for promotion anyway. |

**Written Exercise:** *(a) 'The new word-processing machine not only improves the quality of the letters we send and increases productivity, it gives a daily printout of each operator's total output'. (b) 'I don't like the new equipment. Because I did 28 easy pieces of work one day it has set my quota at 28 per day. I try to get 14 done by lunchtime but I get very nervous – I'm frightened of falling behind'. (c) 'I'm leaving. That machine sets too high*

```
Memo to:   All clerical staff                    Date:  1 July 19--
From:      Organisation and Methods Department
_____

Following the memo from Mr Hughes earlier this week, the word processing
investigation will start on Monday next.  All clerical staff are
required to take an extra copy of all memos, letters, reports etc pro-
duced in the two weeks commencing 4 July and 11 July.  These should be
placed in a file cover labelled WP Investigation and showing your own
name.  On each piece of work please add the following coding, as near
to the top right hand corner as possible.

A.................. This is the author's name i.e. who sent you the work.
P.................. This is the process used to produce the work - i.e.
                    copy typing, audio-typing, word processor, original
                    composition by yourself from notes etc
Rec................ Received at ......... time received
Ret................ Returned at ......... time returned

Any comments or notes may be added if you wish.

Please include all rejected or re-typed letters so that the full extent
of your work is appreciated.

Thank you for your cooperation.      Rita Griffiths
                                     WP Project Teamleader
```

**Fig. 15.1  A memo from Organisation
and Methods Department**

*a standard. I'm fed up with its daily report on my efforts. It can't tell an
easy job from a hard one'.*
**What do these three reports tell us about the problems of introducing new
technology into offices.**

*Go over the topic again until you are sure of all the answers. Then tick it
off on the check list at the back of the book.*